# Fruits and Vegetables

**Carrie Branigan**
**and Richard Dunne**

A+

Smart Apple Media

First published in 2004 by Franklin Watts
96 Leonard Street, London EC2A 4XD

Franklin Watts Australia
45–51 Huntley Street, Alexandria NSW 2015

Editor: Kate Newport, Art director: Jonathan Hair, Designer: Michael Leaman
Design Partnership, Line illustrator: Jeremy Leaman, Consultant: Gill Matthews,
nonfiction literacy consultant and Inset trainer

Picture credits:
Alamy: 14br. Nigel Cattlin/Holt Studios: front cover below, 11tl, 11bl, 12cl,
14cr, 16, 18, 19br, 21b, 22l, 22c, 22r, 23. Alan & Linda Detrick/Holt Studios: 10cl.
Bob Gibbons/Holt Studios: 11cr. Goodshoot/Alamy: 14bl.
Chinch Gryniewicz/Ecoscene: 12bl. Nick Hawkes/Ecoscene: 8.
Willem Harnick/Holt Studios: 6, 7, 11br, 19tl, 20. Peter Landon/Ecoscene: 19tr.
Rosie Mayer/Holt Studios: 23c. Sally Morgan/Ecoscene: 17tr, 24.
Sea Spring Photos/Ecoscene: 10br, 23tl. Ivor Speed/Holt Studios: 10bl.
Inga Spence/Holt Studios: 14cl, 15t, 15c. John Veltorn/Holt Studios: 21t.
Peter Wilson/Holt Studios: 17tl. Picture research: Diana Morris.
All other photography by Ray Moller.

Published in the United States by Smart Apple Media
2140 Howard Drive West, North Mankato, Minnesota 56003

Library of Congress Cataloging-in-Publication Data

Branigan, Carrie.
Fruits and vegetables / by Carrie Branigan and Richard Dunne.
p. cm. — (World of plants)
ISBN 1-58340-613-1
1. Fruit—Juvenile literature. 2. Vegetables—Juvenile literature. 3. Botany—Juvenile literature.
I. Dunne, Richard. II. Title. III. Series.

QK660.B82 2005
575.6'7—dc22

2004059957

2 4 6 8 9 7 5 3 1

# Contents

# Fruits and Vegetables

**Fruits** and **vegetables** are parts of plants. The fruits and vegetables we eat are very good for us.

▲ We eat many different fruits and vegetables.

Look at the picture above. Which do you think are fruits, and which are vegetables? Some foods we eat are not fruits or vegetables. See if you can spot the one that doesn't fit.

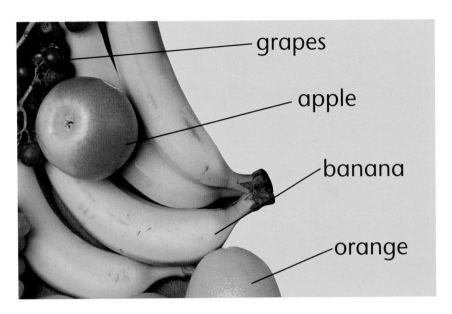

grapes

apple

banana

orange

▷ These are the fruits.

spinach

spring onion

carrot

onion

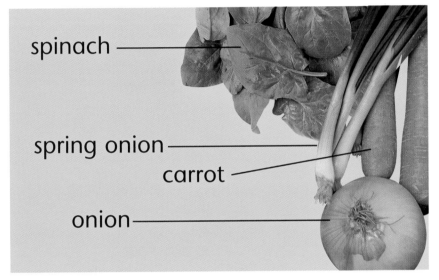

◁ These are the vegetables.

People often think that mushrooms are vegetables because they grow in the ground. This is not true; they belong to another group of living things called **fungi**.

# What Is a Fruit?

Fruits are the parts of a plant that have **seeds** inside them. Some fruits taste sweet.

◀ Apples grow on trees.

▶ If an apple is cut in half, you can see the seeds.

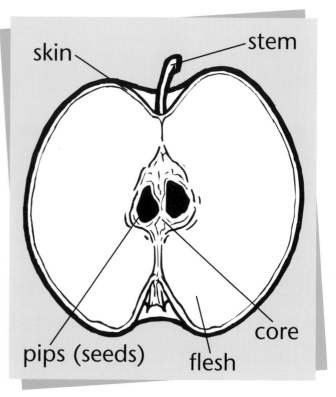

skin — stem

pips (seeds)  flesh  core

We usually eat the **skin** and **flesh** of an apple but leave the core and pips.

Tomatoes are the fruits of a tomato plant. When we eat tomatoes, we eat the skin, the flesh, and the seeds.

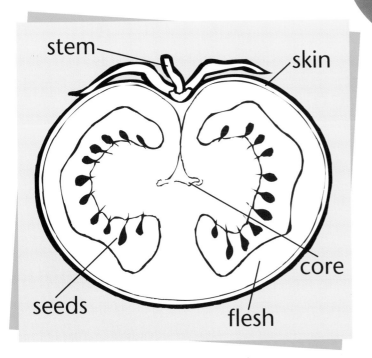

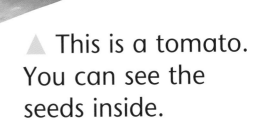

▲ This is a tomato. You can see the seeds inside.

▼ Here are some other sweet fruits that we eat.

Can you name these fruits?

# Seeds We Can Eat

We eat seeds that grow inside fruits. Peas, beans, and **nuts** are all seeds.

A pea **pod** is a fruit because it has seeds called peas inside.

◀ A pea plant with pea pods growing on it.

▶ Peas inside their pod.

▲ Beans are seeds. They grow inside a bean pod.

bean (seed)

pod (fruit)

Nuts are seeds that are found inside
a hard case called a **shell**. Peanuts
and hazelnuts are seeds we can eat.

nut (seed)

shell (fruit)

shell (fruit)

▼ Peanuts grow under
the ground on a peanut
plant.

▼ Hazelnuts grow on
a hazelnut tree.

Can you name other seeds that we eat?

# Grains Are Seeds

Wheat, oats, barley, corn, rice, and rye are all seeds that are called **grain**. Grain is important because we use it to make many different foods.

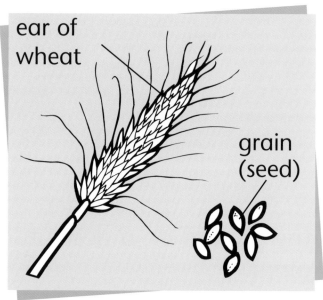

ear of
wheat

grain
(seed)

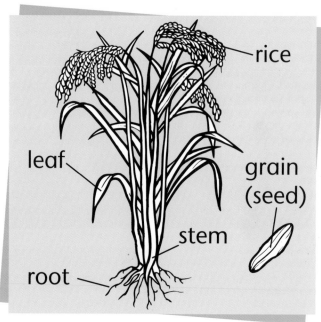

rice

leaf

grain
(seed)

stem

root

Bread is made from flour. Flour is made by grinding wheat or another grain into a fine powder.

▲ Look carefully at this bread, and you can see the grains.

Breakfast cereals are made from lots of different types of grain.

Look at the list of ingredients on a cereal box. How many different grains are there?

# Dried Fruits

Some soft, fleshy fruits can be eaten when they are dried. Dried fruits are very useful because they last longer than fresh fruits.

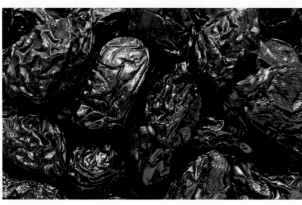 

▲ When plums are dried, they become prunes.

▲ When green grapes are dried, they become sultanas.

When black grapes are dried, they become raisins or currants.

Other dried fruits you can eat are apricots, figs, and bananas. They are sometimes used in breakfast cereals and cakes.

raisin                    sultana

A fruitcake contains many different types of dried fruits.

How many dried fruits can you find in a fruitcake?

# Fruits and Seeds We Don't Eat

Some trees grow fruits that we can eat, such as plums and peaches. Other trees have fruits and seeds that are too hard to eat.

◀ We cannot eat the fruits of a sycamore tree.

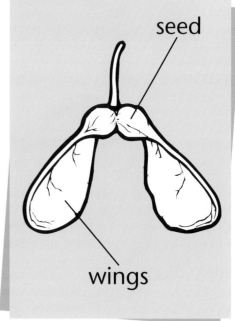

seed

wings

Sycamore tree fruits look like wings. When they fall from the tree, they float and twirl down to the ground.

▲ The outside of a horse chestnut fruit is prickly.

The seed is very hard. ▶

seed (conker)

▶ The fruit of a pine tree is a very hard **cone**.

fruit (cone)

Look at trees at the end of summer and in the fall. When do fruits fall off trees?

# What Is a Vegetable?

The parts of a plant that are not fruits are vegetables. When we eat vegetables, we are eating parts of a plant.

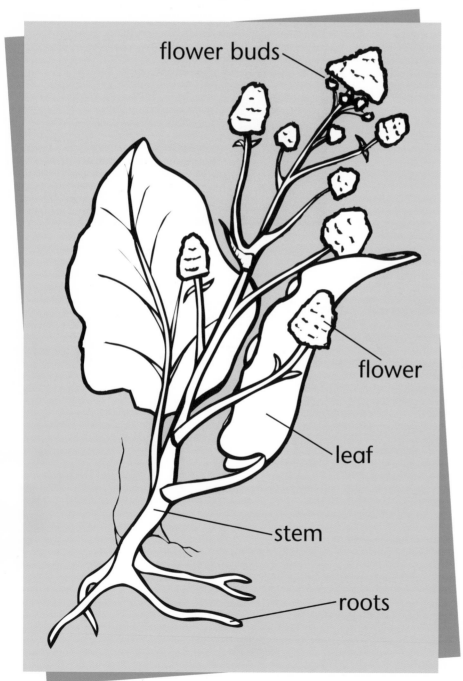

flower buds

flower

leaf

stem

roots

◄ This drawing shows the different parts of sprouting broccoli.

See if you can figure out which parts of these plants we eat. Do you know what the parts are called?

cauliflower

celery

spinach

parsnip

Visit the supermarket and look at all of the vegetables. Try to figure out which parts of the plants they come from.

# Flowers and Stems

We can eat the **flowers** and **stems** of some plants.

When you eat cauliflower or broccoli, you are eating the **flower buds**.

▶ A cauliflower

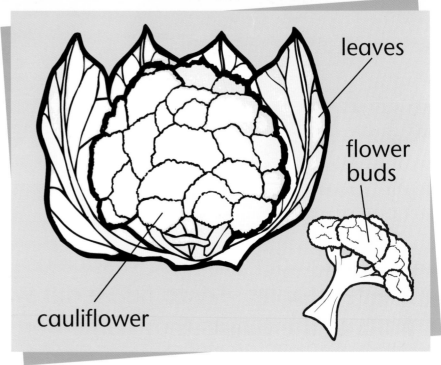

leaves

flower buds

cauliflower

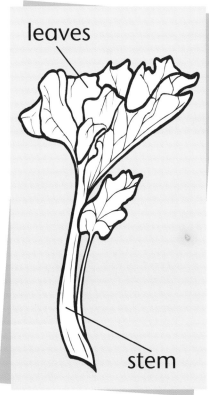

leaves

stem

When you eat rhubarb, you are eating the stem. We cannot eat the **leaves** because they are **poisonous**.

▲ Rhubarb

▼ Asparagus

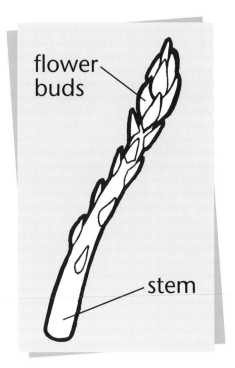

flower buds

stem

When you eat asparagus, you are eating the stem and flower buds.

When you eat a leek, what part of the plant are you eating?

# Leaves We Can Eat

We can eat the leaves of some plants.

▲ Spinach          ▲ Red cabbage          ▲ Brussels
                                            sprouts

When you eat spinach, red cabbage, and
brussels sprouts, you are eating the leaves.

We eat lettuce leaves. Look carefully and you can see the **veins** on the leaves.

lettuce leaf

leaf veins

stem

Look at some other leafy vegetables. Can you see the veins in their leaves?

# Roots We Can Eat

We can eat the **roots** of some plants. Roots store food for the plant.

◀ When you eat carrots or turnips, you are eating the root of the plant.

▲ Carrots    ▲ Turnips

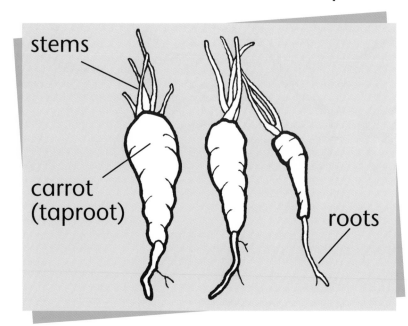

stems

carrot (taproot)

roots

These vegetables are called **taproots**. They are the main root and have smaller roots coming off of them.

new shoots

potato (stem)

People often think that potatoes are roots because they grow under the ground. In fact, potatoes are a type of swollen stem.

▲ A potato plant.

Look at a carrot or a turnip. Can you see where the stem of the vegetable was cut off?

# Healthy Eating

Fruits and vegetables are good for us. We should try to eat at least five types a day.

▶ For breakfast, you could put some fruit on your cereal, such as a banana.

◀ For lunch, you could eat a cheese sandwich with lettuce and tomato.

For dinner, you could eat chicken, potatoes, and beans.

For a snack, you could eat a satsuma.

If you ate all of this, you would have had six different types of fruits and vegetables.

banana
tomato
lettuce
satsuma
bean
potato

Which of these are fruits, and which are vegetables?

27

# Amazing Plants

In 1984, a peach was grown in London, England, that was 12 inches (30 cm) wide. It was bigger than a soccer ball.

The largest watermelon ever was grown in 1980 in Arkansas. It weighed 198 pounds (90 kg)—as much as a large man.

An enormous turnip was grown in Humberside, England, in 1972. It weighed just over 35 pounds (16 kg)—as much as a five-year-old child.

## Use this book to find the answers to this Amazing Plants quiz!

- What are mushrooms?

- Can you name three types of sweet fruits?

- Where do peas grow?

- What is flour made from?

- What is a prune?

- On what tree would you find fruit with wings?

- Where do potatoes grow?

- How many helpings of fruits and vegetables should you eat every day?

# Glossary

**cone**   type of fruit that is found on conifer trees.

**flesh**   soft inner part of fruit or vegetable that we eat.

**flower buds**   flower before it is fully opened.

**flowers**   parts of a plant that are usually very colorful. The flower becomes the fruit and seed of a plant.

**fruits**   parts of a plant that grow from the flower and protect the seed or seeds.

**fungi**   a group of living things (including mushrooms, toadstools, and yeast) that grow on other living things. One of the group on its own is called a fungus.

**grain**   cereal plant that is grown for food.

**leaves**   parts of a plant that are usually green. Leaves use sunlight, air, and water to make food for the plant.

**nuts**   fruits with hard shells that grow on some trees.

**pips**   hard seeds in fruits.

**pod**   type of fruit on some plants, such as bean and pea plants.

**poisonous**   something that will make you sick if you eat or touch it.

**roots**   parts of a plant that hold the plant in the soil. The roots take up water from the soil.

**seeds**   small parts made in the flower of a flowering plant. When seeds are planted, new plants grow from them.

**shell**   hard casing that protects the seed.

**skin**   outer covering of a fruit or vegetable.

**stems**   parts of a plant that hold up the leaves and flowers. The stem carries water from the roots to the leaves.

**taproots**   main roots of a plant with smaller roots growing off of it.

**vegetables**   parts of a plant that are not the fruit, such as the flowers, stems, leaves, or roots.

**veins**   thin tubes in leaves that carry moisture around the plant.

# Index